What We Are Made Of

poems by

Laurie Elizabeth Lambert

Finishing Line Press
Georgetown, Kentucky

What We Are Made Of

Copyright © 2019 by Laurie Elizabeth Lambert
ISBN 978-1-63534-839-2 First Edition
All rights reserved under International and Pan-American Copyright Conventions. No part of this book may be reproduced in any manner whatsoever without written permission from the publisher, except in the case of brief quotations embodied in critical articles and reviews.

ACKNOWLEDGMENTS

The author acknowledges these journals for publication of versions of the following poems:

Bent and Shift—*For a Better World*, 2015; Chocolate is a woman's song—*Clarify*, Literary-Recipe Anthology 2015; Thirst—*The Sycamore*, Summer 2016; Being Human—*For a Better World*, 2016; Chime—*The Sycamore*, Fall 2016; In the Deep of Winter, Praise to a Winter Morning—*Halcyon Days*, 2016 Issue 4; Dear Bugs—*Common Threads*, 2016; A Tissue and a Bandaid, Shouting Poem—*For a Better World*, 2017; Weeding the Labyrinth—*For a Better World*, 2018

I'm deeply grateful for the editing skills and patience of Elizabeth Bourque Johnson; for the nurturing of this collection by Hannah Kelling and Claire Kelling; for long walks and talks with Owen Kelling; for the friendship and feedback of Mary, Mary, Mary Ann, Terri and Jane; for the help of many friends at Women Writing for (a) Change; and for the love and support of my Mom, Evelyn Lambert and my anam cara, Mary K Vasterling.

Publisher: Leah Maines
Editor: Christen Kincaid
Cover Art: Laurie Lambert
Author Photo: Prabir K Das, Aseity Creations
Cover Design: Leah Huete

Printed in the USA on acid-free paper.
Order online: www.finishinglinepress.com
also available on amazon.com

Author inquiries and mail orders:
Finishing Line Press
P. O. Box 1626
Georgetown, Kentucky 40324
U. S. A.

Table of Contents

Autumn
What I have made 1
Chime 3
do trees weep 5
Raptor 6
A tissue and a bandaid 7
O Captain 8
Augury 10
Ruby's Tree 11
Staccato 13
tears at the optometrist 15
Coffee, Toast, Butter 17
A plain brown envelope 19
Yours 21

Winter
Queen of the Woods 25
Being Human 27
In the deep of Winter 28
Ghosts in the Kitchen 30
In the Key of Chocolate 33
Praise to a winter morning 34
Shift 36
At the Kitchen Table with Evelyn 37
The stories we tell 40
On My Dresser 41
Shouting Poem 43

Spring
Spawn 47
Thirst 48
Springtime 49
my river, my darling 50
Bent 52
Rosie 53
Learn 54
that old shirt 55

Eclosing 57
everything else 58
Bluebird 60
One 62
I am listening 64

Summer
Dear Bugs 69
Something Fearsome 70
Cleaning the Closet 71
Brushstroke 72
Linguists 73
Sorting 75
Weeding the Labyrinth 77
A sound not speech 79
Rescue 80
what we are made of 82

*This collection is for my husband, Chris Kelling.
The remarkable life we've made together
is my anchor and my wellspring.*

*we came whirling
out of nothingness
scattering stars
like dust…*

*every atom
turns bewildered*

—Rumi

AUTUMN

What I have made
    after Laurie Kirkpatrick

Lists of things to do,
to which I add things I've already done,
simply for the pleasure of crossing them out.

Many hours of listening.
I'm not sure this is the making of something, but
it is the most valuable thing I have done with my time,
and I am still learning to listen with my whole heart.

Sins.
Oh God have I sinned.
I lifted quarters from my Dad's dresser
to buy cigarettes, while my parents did without
to pay for my asthma medicine. Thank God
I was young and stupid and have those two excuses.
But there are more sins, some I know I will do again,
so I can't be forgiven.
I hope for mercy.

Several good dog lives,
from messy beginnings,
through adventures and naps,
to tender and loving endings.

Three people, two women and a man.
There may have been days
when they wondered about my love
when they were small,
but by now they must be pretty sure.
We take each other for granted, in a good way.

They saved my life, those babies.
I might have fallen off
without the weight of motherhood
to bind me to the world.

A marriage filled with mutual forgiveness.
A messy home, far more beautiful outside than in.

Some good choices
and many mistakes.

Bread, when I was young.
Fudge, when I was old.

Chime

on that branch of the maple
where he often rests
between swoops
for bugs in the grass

bluebird
in the rain

today
in this sogging shower
he is not himself

looking at him out there
looking that way
he is ringing a bell

you never know
where or when
a chime like that
will take you

I blink and find myself
at the side of
my father's casket

he too
was   not
   himself

the color was wrong

like the bluebird

washed out
without vitality
the opposite of vibrant

and yet clearly
there

in the shoulders
slope of the neck
and shape of the head

unmistakably recognized
by eyes, heart, gut

that cherished face, torso
and the way those parts
flowed together
so familiar
so beloved

like this dear bluebird
soggy and gray
and just like my father
in the next instant
gone

do trees weep

these leaves letting go and falling
as the time of stopping approaches

stop growing   stop greening
stop reaching and responding
to sun   air   water

surely a tree in the winter's cold is not
being   a tree
as it is in springtime

blissfully flowering
pitching pollen to the wind
leafing up and breathing

incarnating elation

if I had put my hand   there
on the bark in springtime
would this tree have spoken
the word
    joy

and what word today
as feet crunch
dry brown leaves to dust

as the time of waiting
and slumber
closes in

perhaps
seed

perhaps
hope

Raptor

a hawk is circling outside my window
silent
lower than the treetops
hunting no doubt for a morsel
scampering across the front field

one graceful drop from the sky
is the ending for another of earth's humble beings
scrabbling through the tall grass

reminding me that we all muddle along
with no clairvoyance about our endings

I am left wondering how the hell to get out of bed
carrying this knowing

that all those we love are vulnerable as mice

buttering toast
sifting the mail
picking up a pen

changing the channel
patting the dog
laying down the book

taking off one sock
then the other

glancing out the window

A tissue and a bandaid

Maybe Naomi Shihab Nye
and Kahlil Gibran are right.

Maybe it's true that
we all need to be gouged out,
dug into by sadness before
we can really see and
appreciate the goodness
in the world.

I know, we all know,
there is evil out there.
There are people that are
driven to do harm.
Who knows why,
but they do.
They do harm.

Sometimes the whole world notices,
and sometimes there's just
one person there
to recognize and respond
to the damage that was done.

One person standing there
with a tissue and a bandaid
so we know we're not alone.

One person, reminding us
that we can carry
the kindness of a friend
like a stone in our pocket
to help us remember
there is good in the world.

O Captain

there aren't a lot of houses on this street
maybe a dozen over the mile or so of road
five acre lots mainly, with some up to twenty
mostly plain, nothing fancy

a good place to raise a family
lots of outdoors and no traffic
enough room between you and your neighbor
trees and a creek and plenty of space for a garden

close enough to town but not much of a town really
only two stop lights, good schools
there's milk and bread at the gas station
but it's another five miles to a decent banana

my neighbor's son died yesterday
a worse damn shame you've never seen
the kid was just seventeen years old
moved to this neighborhood when he was three or four
across the street and down a couple houses

he was captain of the high school football team
active in his church, travelled last summer
on a mission trip, sang in the high school choir
got good grades, handsome, tall

he was driving an older convertible
I had seen him before, driving it on our road, grinning
as I would too in a car like that
with the top down on a blue sky summer day

he was driving home after dark last Saturday night
when the car crossed the road, hit the guardrail and a tree
he was airlifted out and lived for almost a week at the hospital
but I don't think he ever opened his eyes

the prayers said on his behalf were in the millions

from his church his school his teams his community
but his brain died after six days sleeping
and not long after his body was let go

 I drive by that spot where it happened every day
it's on my way to and from anywhere I might go

I see the bend in the guardrail and
the gash in the tree, bark torn away
but I can't see how that all happened

I would like to get out of my car
and stand there a while
and just try to figure it out
not even asking the tough question of
why   just the question of how

Augury

Sometimes I have to trust in the world.
To be perfectly honest,
I hate those times,
when I find myself blindly stumbling
in a direction that feels like forward.

I wish that I could reach
across the distance of time
stretch my view into the future
and see for sure
that what I need to be there
is indeed
there.

I would like to be certain
that I can swim this river
that I can get to the other side.

Ruby's Tree

I was walking the field's edge
thinking about the burdens
I was carrying

my children my husband
my mother my friends
all of their sorrows and challenges

and my own fears
my own loneliness
helplessness

I came upon the lone maple
and suddenly I missed my old dog
with an unbearable acuteness
a tremendous weight on my chest

I stopped to catch my breath
by Ruby's tree

the whole of her beloved body
Ruby
was put in the ground
under this now sacred maple

I have been up close to death
I have seen the shuddering last breath
a guttering candle

I have watched the light go out for
beloved companions

and I know too the nature of molecules
the fate of flesh reduced to pieces
strings of carbon nitrogen oxygen
water

my dog Ruby
buried some seventeen years ago
is now in the branches of that tree
figuratively
literally
biochemically

So there I leaned my head
against Ruby's tree
I wrapped my arms around
and leaned

I leaned and let my tears
come out

I felt that tree
press back against me
and hold me up

Staccato

These woods are rarely silent,
no matter the season, full of winged lumberjacks,
harvesting the trees without tumbling them,
pecking them to bits.
Fragments fall on the path at my feet.

There is a symphony here
and I would like to know who and which,
recognize each thrumming note
by the name of bird and tree.

Finding a seat on a downed trunk,
I listen to this wooden xylophone
and tongue drum ensemble, and wish
I could see all the players arrayed
above and around me.

Near to me or far, head-high or in the canopy,
finding nourishment, making shelter,
beating the head-battering song
they are destined to sing, creating in these woods
a concert for my curious and grateful ears.

I know their flight, swooping,
scalloped, wings out and then tucked.
All woodpeckers fly like this.
I know the trees here for them to strike
oak, walnut, maple, ash, sycamore.

I know the Pileated's cry, the racket
of her chatter. Her red cap and jaunty crest,
the sleek black wings and white chest
of this giant. That beak, long and thick,
makes a singular thwack, and then another.
Her holes in our swing set were gaping, earnest.
The bass drum's beat in these woods,
low and resonant, that's her.

I am familiar too with the trill
of the Red-Bellied woodpecker
and his look in the air.
He comes to our feeder daily
and I admire the bright brushstroke
on his top and subtler one on his tummy.
Is that him I hear today, slamming
his bill into a soft spot on a dying ash,
dining on the root of the tree's demise?

I know as well the timid and small Downy,
looking dashing in black and brilliant white,
checks and stripes, small red hat.
I am lucky to get a look
when I offer peanuts and she accepts.
Perhaps today, having found a perch
on a great hollow tree, she is herself surprised
at the echo of her stroke in these woods.

tears at the optometrist

Today at the eye doctor's office, the technician took a picture of the back of my eye.
She positioned me just right in front of a machine and said
"open reallllly wide"
and
"look look look, okaaaay and Blink."

After that, she took me back to the examination room and sat me down.
Fiddled with the computer and put the picture on the screen
of my two eyes, left and right.
Then she departed, leaving me alone in the room.

I leapt out of my seat to have a closer look.

It looked like Mars.
All red and orange
with interconnected reddish rivers and streams
and a whitish hole
a grayish bump.

And it seemed wrong to be looking at my eye with my eye,
you know what I mean?

On the screen, of course,
the eye was huge,
and in my face, in my head,
quite small.

I could see my eyelashes at the edges of the picture,
and I was glad that I didn't wear mascara.

And I felt the wonder of this event,
that this is where we have come to,
that a stranger can take a picture of the inside of my eye
and show it to me.

And I started to cry a little,
that the mystery and miracle was changing in this way.

It was the second time I had cried at the optometrist.

When I first pulled in to the parking lot,
there were ginkgos everywhere,
teenager ginkgo trees,
two no taller than I am,
all autumn yellow and gorgeous.

I opened my car door
and there was a perfect buttery leaf
right there on the asphalt.

And I stayed in the car
and shut the door.
I felt my heart quake some
and let a few tears fall.
I was early for my appointment anyway.

I got out
and walked around the parking lot,
stood looking at each of those young and hopeful ginkgo trees,
admiring and appreciating each in turn,
up close.

And then I went in.
And the inside of my eye was revealed to me.

 What next.
What next will pull water and salt from my ducts
to dribble down my face
in helpless surprise and gratitude.

I am ready,
I am here with my heart
cracked open,
waiting.

Coffee, Toast, Butter

When my Mom comes to visit, she always starts the day slowly. She moves from the bed to the kitchen, gathers what she needs to start her day. Bread, butter, jam, instant coffee, mug, spoon, sugar bowl, knife. She places some items on the kitchen table and others on the counter. Coffee, such as it is (Nescafe), is stirred and placed in the microwave to go through the 'beverage' cycle not once but twice. While the coffee is coming to a boil she starts the toast. Due to the vagaries of my toaster, it too needs to be toasted twice.

Finally, with scorching coffee and crunchy toast she sits at the head of the table and begins the buttering. First, the toast must cool a little bit because she does not want the butter to melt. It needs to stay hard and solid and cool, like cheese. Her slices of butter are thick as the pats you get in restaurants and she arranges them artfully on the toast, side by side, cutting in half if needed to completely fill the whole surface.

She bites then, satisfaction filling her face as she chews, slowly. The eating of two pieces of toast could take half an hour, perhaps more. Conversation will be sprinkled in, and that will take up some time, but the chewing and swallowing also are unhurried. It's often a couple of hours before the coffee and toast are gone and the morning kitchen stories are told.

We mosey to her bedroom together to make the bed, carefully, smoothing all the wrinkles from the sheets. After it's so meticulously made, I sit on the bed and she walks to the dresser to get her pills and hands them to me. The bed is tall, and she is not, so she does a sort of lean/lift/half-hearted sideways throwing of her body up onto the bed to join me. We sort the collection of prescription pills and supplements and double-check to be sure all are accounted for. I hand her the glass of water that has spent the night at her bedside, and again we have the careful and slow swallowing. There follows more chatter, stories, laughter before we each gracelessly dismount our opposite sides of the bed and begin to contemplate showering. It's probably creeping toward noon.

My Mom says
she has no "hurry"
no "make it snappy"
no "hop to it"
or "on the double."

Now, at 88,
she has lots of
"just a minute" and
"wait a while" and
"I'm getting there."

Things take time.
That's just the way it is.

This is how each day begins when my Mom comes to my house. I pull out all my patience and then some. I call off everything that I am able to cancel for every day she is here. I put my "hurry up" in the closet and lock the door.

a plain brown envelope

I went to the Post Office down in town
late on a Saturday morning
hoping to make it before they closed
at noon.

I had stuffed some stuff
into a large brown envelope.
A couple of bank statements still coming
to your permanent home address
a late graduation card with a check inside, I think
a blank journal with unlined pages for drawing or writing
or both.

I had not found the time to write a letter,
though I had found the time to read
hundreds of pages of novels.
I didn't know what to say except I miss you
I miss you I miss you I miss you.
Nine hundred miles. Why so far
so soon.

I put a poem and a short essay in there
from my recent writings.
One you may have already seen,
one so recent you can't have.
Neither particularly impressive,
but I was there,
in those words.

I stood at the counter in the lobby of the USPS
with the envelope, putting on the return address
and it felt wrong somehow to send those things
like that.

I started searching my pockets
and my bag, adding things
a lucky penny

two hair ties
a heart-shaped stone
a hanky that my mother gave me
white with blue crocheted trim.

I started crying softly
and a lady came in, emptied
her PO Box and stood next to me
at the counter, sorting her mail and
forcing me to stifle my snuffling
as I tried to fit my whole heart in a
plain
brown
envelope.

I licked the flap
went inside to the postman
handed over my soul
and seven dollars
fifty-three cents.

Yours

Was it because I wanted a person of my own
wanted someone who
belonged to me

without knowing then
that it wouldn't always be so
or even ever be so

well, maybe briefly
in that period of utter helplessness for you
and complete responsibility for me

but then less and less so
until finally it is not you who are mine
but I who belong entirely to you

when you are gone
when I have reluctantly
oh so very unbearably
let go

you are no longer
and perhaps
were never mine

But I belong to you
helplessly
endlessly

yours

WINTER

Queen of the Woods

standing at the top of the ridge
gazing into the river bottoms
I see between me and the water
the sycamores
tallest and whitest
of the winter tree skeletons

after the rains this past summer
they swelled and split their bark
molting shards of stiff and brittle skin

slabs of thick gray paper
fell to the ground

pelts were shed
into the river

***

how do my towering friends
endure this bursting growth

weight of water
tearing the rind

blanched underlayer
exposed and vulnerable

surviving only if
they weather
this rupture

***

praise then for winter
the respite

the white giant sycamores
resting

collecting the will
the readiness
to swell
to crack again

Being Human

It's a hard time to be a human being
The world seems to be losing kindness
In its place antipathy, violence, blood
How do we hold on to hope

Who will stand for love, who will say
We are all brothers and sisters, who will speak for
Trees, rivers, elephants, whales, sparrows, bees
The world seems to be losing kindness

All the stories we hear tumble together
Blood on the street here, there, and again
In another place too, hatred has won
How do we hold on to hope

A hand reaching out, pulling a stranger under the table
This rescue, this kindness comes in response
To blood on the street, here, there, and again
Where is everyday altruism, where is love

In its place antipathy, violence, blood
The hand reaching out to help a stranger
Is too late, the beating heart is stilled
In another place, again, hatred has won

All the stories we hear tumble together
Who will save us all from those who find victory
In death of self and other. Where is grace
How do we hold on to hope

Vote for life, for love, with your hands, your voice
your feet, your breath. Choose kindness.
Be the hand reaching out to help a stranger
It's a hard time to be a human being

In the Deep of Winter

brittle cold howling winds
one pair of socks is not enough
and at night the sheets are cold

the doorknob sticks and cold rushes in
as the dogs dash out
barking to return in barely an instant

the long view from the window
is dull, frost on the sill
inside and out, gray sky
white scrambled snow
leafless tree skeletons
a few brave evergreens

but here closer in
dozens of birds at the feeder
bright red of cardinals
brilliant against the white backdrop
rust of the rufous-sided towhee
eye-catching and bright as he hops
the spot on the dove too more blue
in this frigid bland world

time for a walk surely
to get the blood moving
preparations are daunting
adding layer after layer
by the time I am ready
the dogs are frantic

twenty paces across the yard
ice forms on my eyelashes
crunching and breaking the crust
that tops the snow up to my ankles
the dogs' breaths caught
white on their chins

we trudge through the whiteness
looking down at the tracks
of bird and rabbit
deer squirrel coyote
their diaries here at my feet

down the hillside in the woods
punching the snow
with my sidewise boot
using an improvised walking stick
to keep from sliding

I can see through the woods
to the river bottom and beyond
all white all frozen and brittle
save the river streaming still

we are drawn to the water's edge

ice lines the river's banks
frozen sculptures in the slushy water
whorls and curves in the ice
with bubbles flowing by underneath

for a moment I forget I am cold

until a dog clumsily shatters
the objects of my attention

throwing snowballs and laughing
as the dogs catch them in their mouths
surprised at their crunch and disappearance
we head back to the house

up the hill for tea and treats
more window television
with birds on every channel

Ghosts in the Kitchen

Making fudge on a cold gray afternoon
by myself in the kitchen.
Carole King is singing holiday songs.
I am puttering along stirring
and watching for that magic transition
from bubbling goo
to snappy pre-fudge.
Waiting for that instant
when I need to add the chips and vanilla
and stir like a maniac
until all the little lumps have disappeared
into a thick soup of deep brown.
Then just as speedily pour
into the butter-greased pans,
and nudge the mass into the corners
before it's solid.

It's a lot of waiting and stirring and then a race against time my friends.

When all this is over, I run a butter knife
along the sides of the pan, putting the scrapings
from this first batch in a bowl.
That's when I realize I am not alone. Lord, there are so many
ghosts in this kitchen that I sit down to pay attention.

My children are off at college, but still they're here with me
pushing past me for the bowl full of scrapings
from the pan, hot hot hot! Quick into the mouth
and sitting on the tongue, lips held open panting
trying to cool down that hot delicious chocolateness.

I'm making fudge today so it'll be here waiting
when the first one gets home on Friday.
She wrote yesterday that she really missed me.
I wrote back "Darlin, I am holding you so tight
in my heart right now I can hardly tell you're not here."

My Dad's in the kitchen too,
he's been gone from this world for decades,
but the sound of the knife against the pan draws him to me.
My Mom always put the fudge pan scraps
in his lunchbox, if she could keep us kids from eating them.
She often made fudge while we were at school, maybe that's why.

My Dad, he was besotted with love
for the grandchildren who were lucky enough
to know him before he passed, so he joins us here.
This morning his mouth is watering but he stands back
smiling, and lets the kids have it all.
Big-hearted, Big-loving, God and Family kind of man.
God I miss that man.

Of course, my Mom's been here with me
since I started putting out the ingredients.
I could call her on the phone,
but I hear her voice in my head
so clearly that I don't bother. When I was a child
she would make upwards of 40 pounds of fudge
each Christmas season. It was her gift to everyone,
neighbors, aunts&uncles, my Dad's coworkers,
the postman, teachers, everyone.
They all got fudge from Evelyn
and praised the Lord for their good fortune.

She tried to show me the secret,
how things looked and sounded and felt
when everything was just right
and it was time to add the chips. But I never got it.
I don't think I ever wanted to get it.
I wanted her to make the fudge.

But when I moved to Ohio, I had to learn.
She visited and showed me again.
I made chocolate soup.

She showed me yet again,
and I made chocolate cement.
Finally, I got a candy thermometer
and between the two of us we figured how
Laurie could make creamy lovely fudge
using a little technology.

But this morning, I don't need a thermometer,
I am feeling everything in my bones, in my blood,
beating and pumping in my heart
stirring and stirring, watching the pan
and watched by the eyes of my ghostly companions.
My Mom whispers in my ear when the time is right.

In the Key of Chocolate

chocolate is a woman's song

truffles, cake
brownies, pudding
cookies, fudge

Pie

the whisper of the knife
in the delicate, artful act
of removing the first slice

the whistle
of the canned whipped cream
embellishing

the scrape of the spoon
gathering the last morsel
to your lips

a wish
to make your soul dance

a hope
to bring comfort

mother's hymn
friend's blues ballad
lover's lullaby

chocolate sings darling,
beloved, sweetheart, dearest

chocolate is a woman's song
of love

take this
and eat of it

Praise to a winter morning

Praise to these cozy flannel sheets
myself snugged in, coming to awareness.
The warm weight on my thigh
of my Labrador's head, her breaths deep
and long, warbling a low note in her throat.
I slither out to turn up the heat
and slide back in listening to the delightful
whooshing of warm air rushing from the vent.
Waiting for the house to move from sixty degrees
to something more friendly.

Praise these moments, the day not yet begun
on the edge of everything that will come to pass.
Seeing the light arriving at the window,
feeling the smooth fur under my hand now
as she thumps a slow dawning wag,
my dreams fleeing, even as I try to bring them
forward to my attention.
We rise, my dog and I, and the day begins.
The hot tea warms my hands on the sides of the mug,
the first sip sliding across my tongue,
so welcome as it passes my sleep-parched throat.

Praise to the smell of toast and melting sharp cheddar,
the satisfying crunching both in my mouth
and the dog's as she gobbles her kibble. She finishes first,
places her head on my lap knowing,
knowing as sure as it's morning,
that the last bite of this cheesy toast is hers.
Across the table birds are visiting the feeders,
better than the morning paper, they tell me what I need to know.
It's brisk, there's a wind.

Praise this start to a day, this dog, this tea, this toast.
There are other more hurried and troubled ways
for days to begin than this.

This ease, this pleasure, these moments that make a life,
that make me want to draw breath again and again
and see what happens next,
grateful and wanting, both.

Shift

the world is not the same
from one heartbeat to the next

even breathing
changes the composition of things

oxygen in, carbon dioxide out
and the planet is altered

when you and I meet
share words, ideas, feelings
and our eyes, ears and souls focus
on each other

voila

the moment before we spoke
we were this
and then

never this again

At the Kitchen Table with Evelyn

I've reached the age of losing things.
I have always been pretty good at forgetting
but now I forget really hard.
My brain seems to effortlessly work
to erase, conceal
obliterate.

I am learning ways to cope
with forgetting and losing.
One way is to just let go.
But I am much better at holding on
persisting doggedly
digging in.

Driving myself crazy
that's how it ends up.
Bellowing my frustration
and causing my poor dogs to
hide under the kitchen table.

Recently a new strategy worked for me.
Oddly enough it was a technique
I've been telling my kids to use for years.

It involves a sort of mental time travel,
with intentional relaxation.
A return to the moments around
the last time you saw that thing,
reliving them in your mind.

Not with any desperation
but with a calm centeredness,
an easy purposefulness
absent anxiety or fear.

That fear that you will never find
that thing.

I lay in my bed in the dark last night,
restless after many hours of searching
my room, my office, my bags,
my files and even my suitcase
for a note from my mother.

She gave it to me during a recent visit
and I needed
I really really needed
to know where it was.
But it didn't seem to be anywhere.

Fretting in my bed, I remembered
what I'd advised my kids to do
when something was lost.

In my mind, I returned
to the kitchen table
where my mother and I both sat.

My Mom, with a pen and paper, was making
a list for me of things to remember,
things she wanted me to know about,
things I would need to know when she died.

These things were hard to talk about
for both of us, but I knew
she was giving me a gift.
This list was meant to make it easier,
gentler for me, in the future.

(And I had lost it.)

But, as I lay there, dreaming myself back
to her kitchen table, I saw her tear the
pages from the pad and hand them to me,
her face serious, sincere, loving.

And I felt myself getting up from my chair
walking to the guest room and folding
the sheets to just the right size
so they would fit inside
a zippered compartment
in my wallet.

And then, I fell asleep.

This morning I woke up,
ate my toast and drank my tea
fed the dogs and let them out
and back in and read a few pages
of a good and captivating novel.

Eventually I reached into my backpack
held the wallet in my hands
opened the zipper
and there they were
those pages
in my Mom's beloved and
almost indecipherable left-handed script.

The stories we tell

We are shaped by the words
we wrap around our souls
fastened and formed
by invisible threads.

We create a quilt of stories
with the fabrics
of our mind's recollections
our heart's narratives.

There are spaces too for the tales
our mothers tell about us,
adventures our children recall,
moments captured by the anam cara,
and the lovers' versions of history.

We are patched, repaired, remade
again and again as we claim
the stories we hear about our lives
intermingled with those memories
we share with the world.

All sewn against the backing
of the truths we voice
only to ourselves.

On My Dresser

the baby teeth, fairy notes,
little brown horse,
the folded-up pages of "I will not hit my sister"
and string of beads that spells 'Mom'

the swath of my own towhead locks
now over 50 years old, still curled,
the locket with entwined hearts
bearing my parents' initials,
and earrings that were my Nana's

I know I have seen remnants like these
at antique malls, garage sales
No doubt countless treasures
are in landfills

I shudder to think of it

Yes, I kissed the little brown horse
remembering my child holding
her most treasured possession

Yes, I tried on my Nana's earrings
conjuring the perfume
she dabbed behind her lobes

I'm counting my good fortune
in these memories
Yes

But wishing for the past too

the time
when I was the most important person
in my child's life

the time

when my mother and father
were enjoying life together

It's going to take some hopefulness
some work and some luck
if the next part of my life
is to be as priceless as my past

I cleaned my dresser, I sorted
I kissed more objects

I started the work
of moving into my future

Shouting Poem

I have decided to stop tip-toeing
and to never
whisper
again.

No more screaming in my car where
no one can hear me and
I don't bother anybody with
my breaking heart.

I have decided to stop silently
weeping, blubbering
into a little paper tissue
squashed into a ball
in my hands.

I am going to howl now
and scream
and carry a large towel
and loudly blow my nose as
tears wash down my face.

I am done with hiding
with discretion
with wondering if
this or that is okay
and asking permission
and forgiveness.

I am so done with all that.

I am ready to be naked
in the street,
my naked feelings on display
along with my sagging breasts
my flat ass

and my slouching
tired shoulders.

I am going to light a candle
and another and another
and not be afraid anymore
that my house will burn down
God help me, if it's going to burn
I want to know how it happened
I can be the one
that sparked the flame.

SPRING

Spawn

motion at the river's edge
mermaid tails
flashing

golden fans
with bright redbrown spots
glowing in a sunbeam

a pinwheel spinning
in and out of the water

tubular silver fish
as thick as and longer than my arm

churning over one another
a swirling shining mass
flowing from those glimmering
twirling tails

synchronized watery ballet
primal urgent aquatic orgy

dance of life
slippery
ghostly
fleeting
holy

Thirst

honeybee lands on the lip
of a Morning Glory
a deep purple vase
and pauses there

then climbs in
deep, deeper
and disappears

I want that

I want that elemental thirst
and the finding of something
that will quench it

and most of all
the climbing down
into the deepness
and vanishing

Springtime

if a flower could sing a song
the trout lily would offer
a hymn   or two

first, to the night sky
shy petals folded in prayer
chanting humble supplications

second, to the sun
stretching open to show a star's reflection
shouting joyful notes of praise

***

if a flower could sing a song
the trillium would perform
in three-part harmony
children's choir, a mob in green and white

weeks later
a mellow note of grace
blushing beauty of aging
brightening in the face of demise

my river, my darling

The river has changed again this year.
The rains have been heavy,
the floods intense and filled
with lumber and duff.

Much has been moved around.

Once the debris has settled,
the water has a mind, a will
of its own and goes
where it wishes.

A new rush and tumble,
a fresh island.

When I stand on the ridge
and look down at the path
my friend now wanders,
I can see she is flowing in places
where there used to be
land or rocks or sand.

The river is diverging
from her old self.

I had hoped that she and I
were of the same mind,
that we wanted the same things.

But now I see that the river and I
may be diverging as well.

I cannot cross here anymore.
I can stand where I used to dive.

Water is flowing in spaces
and in ways that will change

our relationship.

I am still strong enough
to throw a stone, to roll a log, to speak
the language of persuasion
we both understand.

We have had this conversation before,
my river and I, moving with
and around the obstacles placed
by time and weather.

How many times have I laid down
in this water and whispered
thank you my darling.

Bent

All day today I have carried this,
carried her heart. I can feel the weight
straining my shoulders, bending me.

She is the mother of that poor soul
executed by immolation.
I have been carrying her with me
since yesterday, when I was driving
my car and heard a description on the radio
that made my breath stall in my chest.

A cage, a fire, screams.
All recorded and posted with words.
I could not, cannot stop my mind
from seeing, imagining.
I cannot stop my heart from reaching
toward the loved ones of that poor soul.

On my walk through the fields today
I was asking myself Why
not   Why did this happen
but   Why is it that I, half a world away
cannot put this burden down?
   Why am I still bent
still carrying this woman's heart
this loss, this pain, this sorrow
this outrage, this hopelessness.

I cannot put this burden down.

Rosie

Out in the yard with the tennis ball. Over and over, I swing the racket
sending the lemon globe in a long long arc. And she is off, quick as lightning
bounding down the hillside, tripping past the ball as it jumps along
and finally stops. She circles back to grab it in her mouth.

Come Rosie Come! I yell, to get her used to the idea
though I know, called or not, of course she'll come now
for another chance to chase her favorite toy. I kneel
and watch her bobbing toward me, her fluffy yellow
body springing through the tall grass, ears flapping.
That golden triangle with three black dots,
eyes, nose, bouncing up the hill.

I praise and pat her with enthusiasm as she releases
the ball at my feet, my Rosie. She drops to her haunches
close to sitting but not at all at rest. She is instead
nothing but energy and anticipation, every muscle
twitching. Though she doesn't speak to me, I can hear her.
Again, she tells me, *again. Pleeeease. Now!*

And she's off, careening after her treasure. This lucky dog,
with this soft green expanse under her feet, this blue sky day,
this smitten loyal friend watching her pleasure and purpose
and feeling the same. *Yes my dear, again, yes.*

Catching her breath, she lies in the grass as I rub her belly.
This lucky puppy, Rosie.

We both turn when we hear the neighbor's dog begin to bark.
Chained to a stake in the ground
day and night.

Learn

learn
stillness
from the blue heron

silent
weightless landing
on the river bank

self-folding origami

standing profile
locked
thin as a slice of bread

for moments
one—two—three—
then

    lifting

folding and
unfolding into flight

legs bowed
neck pleated

wings opening out
to unthinkable breadth

    no footprint
    in the mud

that old shirt

thank goodness that endings come with beginnings
that the end of this is the beginning of that
one voyage comes to its conclusion
and the next journey begins
not without trepidation surely
but begins nonetheless

sometimes I want to call out
Stop
just stop

let me stay in this part for longer
for even just a bit longer

because I love this part
because I have gotten so delightfully
comfortable in this part

this part feels like a ragged old shirt
that I have worked in and slept in
grieved and danced in
spinning and singing
spilling wine and
tears

why must I take off this stained old shirt
and put on a new one that has creases and
that new shirt smell and tags still on it

will this new shirt soften
and come to caress my body
a second skin

can I put on
courage and hope
fortitude and faith
to wear into the uncertainty

of what lies ahead
like armor
like light

can I find someone
to hold my hand

Eclosing

each day seeking redemption
what can one woman do

butterfly in the grass
a yellow leaf
fluttered by wind

I lift her up in
my cupped hands

I can feel the water
weighting her wings

hearts filled with want
we go together
to find a place

to rest to weep to molt
the millstones that vanish
with metamorphosis

waiting together
for the lift of a breeze

she leaves me

we take a part of each other
into the next beginning

everything else

it's a new phase, this one
there's an intensity
and a thinning of the skin
    the wall has dropped

I see the world
and the world sees me

this rawness
this feeling of all these
    feelings

exhausting work

I used to shrug more
look away more
ignore more and
    ignore better

but now there seems to be
no turning away

tears spilling in my car
at my desk
and walking in my beloved woods

salty waters

longing loneliness love
gratitude wonder nostalgia

all used to be dry feelings
the misty versions
less controlled
but more of everything else
    besides control

is this the new way
that I will be in the world

wet surrender

or is this a temporary space
someplace on my path
that I am passing through

I will need more towels tissues
handkerchiefs

more patience with myself and
forbearance from those
who love me

serene stamina

I have an inkling
a suspicion
that an opening
is opening wider

that more will be let in
and be kept
and also
    keep spilling over

Bluebird

he came back today
I have been looking and looking for weeks
I've seen cardinals, sparrows, woodpeckers,
blue jays that make me turn my head quickly
and then sigh a sigh richly laden with
disappointment

these other birds have even perched on
His branch, just outside the bathroom window

I've seen him in the yard
in the heights of the giant dying ash tree
perching there on a bare branch
and diving to the grass for bugs
but it's not the same

it's not our meeting place
me at the bathroom window
toothpaste slopping on my chin
and the bird on the branch of the maple
where we can say hello
eye to eye

today he was there
for the first time since autumn
and my heart swelled so
I almost moved
I almost spoke
but I stopped myself in time

so he would stay
my blue friend

I can put up with so much more
in the rest of the world
woes, worries, complications
terrors, tragedies and corruption

if I can have this one friend

he saves me from despairing
he gives me hope
flying through each day
with nothing more pressing
or important than the next
nibble, the next gorgeous swoop
down to the earth, back up
to the waiting branch
flashing brilliant sun-struck blue
the best blue
and that red breast
brilliant white belly

should I send a letter to God
and say
dear God
wherever you are
please let me just have this
bluebird
at the upstairs bathroom window
by the sink where I wash my wrinkling
face, brush my worn old teeth
and comb my graying hair

just this bluebird to lift my spirits
and return me to the world
with love for the next moment
and the next

One

Like many friendships
there is a little bit of
taking for granted.

I saw you the day
before yesterday
but not since.
Not today.
Yet somewhere inside
I know
it's nowhere near
the end for us.

Tomorrow, the next day
we'll cross paths again.
I'll see you
and even from a distance
I'll know you.

My heart will lift
in my chest
  a beat ahead
quickening with
yes.

My eyes
my heart my blood
my breath all one
in a response
of gladness and
gratitude.

I know you, my friend.
You and I are
connected by something
I cannot name.

It's love, yes, but more.
Something elemental,
something in my skin,
my tissues, my cells
my atoms and even
the spaces between
those parts.

Something magic
something holy
that makes
of us two
one.

I am listening

a year after I built
my barnyard labyrinth I needed
to plant a ginkgo tree
at the center
it was a kind of needing
not desperate but imperative
certain and urgent

I needed to sit with
a source of ancient wisdom
    in the middle
of my journeys through the labyrinth
to rest in the shade of this living fossil
symbol of loyalty and friendship

I searched for the ginkgo
that was meant for me
found him full of greening buds
and brought him home

dug the hole deep and wide
wheel-barrowed the giant
root ball and dangling sapling
to the center

planted him all by myself
cared for him like a mother
though the weather
during his first year here
was a trial

a scorching hot summer with
rain rain rain
then no rain at all
and temperatures this past winter
prolonged and unreasonably frigid

I sat with him today
and enjoyed the energy and beauty
of his many leafing buds

I saw too the scars
of last summer and winter
branches that are
brittle and budless
I wondered whether it is best
to cut them off
or leave them be

this tree has things to say
about living and growing in the world

pushing down deep and
weathering the weather

bearing that which wounds and disfigures
and living with the scars that follow

waking up and bursting open into space
unfolding in no hurry
with grace and inevitability

sensing what to do and when to do it
from a deep-inside knowledge
older than the dirt his roots entwine

SUMMER

Dear Bugs

dear bugs outside my window

thank you for this evening hymn

I don't know who you are
or what you look like

but that note
you are trilling
is perfect

what if my voice
rang into the darkness
without my name or face
to claim its pitch

what is the sound of
my most primitive request
the music of my nucleus

my fundamental rhythm
thrumming

what song would my soul
send out into the night

Something Fearsome

When held by fear
I remind myself
fear is natural, even
good. Fear fuses
experience, logic, intuition.

When I run away,
cover my head and try to disappear,
fear can keep me safe from harm.

But what of the times when fear
wells up without a palpable cause?
When I feel that clutch at my heart,
stricture of my throat, but
there is nothing.

No smell of smoke
no streak of blood
no strange chest pain
no dog barking at
something outside the door.

I have to go alone, go deep
to pull it into the light.
I have to summon the courage
to touch it, to tease it
apart, to find out
what it's made of,
how it was fashioned
from the stuff of my life,
the cold tangle at my center.

Cleaning the Closet

The dress I wore to my father's funeral has been in a dry cleaner bag in my closet for a quarter century. The delicate color of a chicory flower, it's a silky but not shiny material with tiny white somethings all over it and a waist that drops low in the front, a tie belt that snugs up the back, a modest scoop neck and short sleeves. It's a size four. I could never zip it now. I bought that dress the day after my father died.

He left us, suddenly and completely unexpectedly, when I was in a plane flying to see him for the first time in a year or so. It was the Fourth of July weekend, and I was headed home to celebrate with my family. My husband was along as well, to fete my thirtieth birthday and the first anniversary of our wedding.

I arrived to a nightmare.

My mother, my sisters and I agreed that my Dad would not want his daughters and his wife dressed in black for his funeral. So, we all bought lovely dresses, all pastels. The women of my family were dressed for Easter Sunday on the saddest day of our lives.

I've never worn it again, but there's something about that dress that I just can't give away or discard.

Bury me in a dress like that.

Brushstroke

please paint me near, or better yet, in
water

please too, color the water that delightful
dark blue and gray, with traces of green,
tea-brown, copper and rippling white

above me color the sky a deep and bright blue
with just a few of the whitest kind of puffy,
pillowy clouds

make the water still enough that those clouds are
reflected in its surface slightly wavy and loosened

if I can ask further, though I know I've asked
a lot already, please paint nearby
a tired great blue heron, so weary
that she will stand, still as a stone
for a long, long time

be careful with the brush
to distinguish those darker feathers
tufting on her head and
the many subtle shades of blue and gray
on her folded wings and body

show me
her bended, knobby, graceless knees
and the precision of her long sharp beak

yes please
to all of this
water, almost calm
blue sky, white clouds
great blue heron
and me

Linguists

for days as we kayaked around the lake
we saw the family on the water

two adults, black with white spots,
white band at the neck, long sharp beak
iridescent black head, and those red eyes

and one small puff ball
brown and tan and mostly air I think
in the midst of all that fluff

we would slide on over
toward where they were diving for dinner
and feeding the youngster

watching with binoculars
and trying not to disturb anybody

and then we'd be startled
by that tune
the three note holler

it's an interval of a third I think
and then a further leap
to a sharp fourth or so

a full beat blast of each tone
with perhaps a quarter rest
in between

as we watched,
diving ceased and
the babe was tucked in tight

skyward, there was the other resident beauty

enormous, regal, with white head and tail

dirt brown body and yellow hooked beak
soaring over the scene
and landing in a tall tree on the bank
eyeing the brown downy morsel

our northwoods vacation highlight
was watching as the babe began
tentative head dunks
and then short dives on its own

still dining from the beaks of parents
but learning, changing
its head smoothing
and its fuzziness flattening some

all week, we heard on occasion
the three note song
sometimes from out of sight
across the lake or down the shoreline

our own hearts stopped
as we too scanned
the skies for danger

and every time
there was the white-headed
majestic menace sailing overhead
landing in a tree
and leering

we learned the language
we know now
how to say 'Eagle!' in Loon

Sorting

In the beginning, before the surrender, I sorted.
At the end of each day,
when The Three were tucked away,
I sorted toys into big buckets
as I picked up the detritus
of a day full of children.

Animal
Human
Vehicle
Other

It seemed important. I was a sorter, a scientist
as well as a mother, and perhaps I was clinging
to that part of me that was rational
and had a certain way of understanding,
that focused on identification
and appropriate
pigeonholing.
With each thing in its right context,
in its place with other, like, things,
I felt a sense of control.

I could still embrace the idea
that I had any kind of control.

When my Mom came to visit,
I complained that she didn't fold
the children's clothes quite right.
She dropped
the onesie in her hands
said, "Well I can fix that"
and stopped helping with laundry.
I relented and begged, she resumed
folding in her own way
and it looked a lot better to me.

My Mom saw the way
I was carefully sorting the toys.
Sitting on the floor,
gathering them into a pile within my reach
and then tossing each
into the appropriate collection.
She asked "What on earth are you doing?"
I carefully explained to her,
as if it should be obvious,
and she said "Well I can fix that."
She gathered up the pile in her apron
and dumped into each bucket
until it was full
as I watched with chagrin
and a bit of horror.

"Toys" she said.
"They are not different things,
they are all the same. Toys."

I was sorting for me I suppose.
No, I don't suppose,
I know.

This was the beginning of the long,
perhaps endless process
of learning to yield.

To give up that which does not serve.
Embrace entropy.
Surrender.

Weeding the Labyrinth

I have been working in the labyrinth lately,
rather than walking the circuits.
There's a lot to be done there in the summer,
mostly weeding, it's never finished.

Lately, I think of it as a prayer,
my weeding. As I tug at unwanted,
unsightly, and occasionally prickly green,
it is a prayer for healing.

My own private prayer,
a poor poet's metaphor
to pull the malignant cells
from the body of my friend.

And too, to take out poisonous pieces
from the body of the world.
It is my sacred work,
my only way to pray.

Yesterday I tugged the last weed
from the outermost circuit.
Of course, this meant it was time
to start over in the middle,
where they were once again
poking up their green heads.

But this morning, instead,
I lit a candle and walked.
I entered quiet, though I usually begin
with a chant on my lips.
I wanted to see what would come.

Within the first few steps a song rose in my mind,
and repeated. I listened to a glorious nameless
symphonic rhapsody as I walked, and eventually
I opened my throat and sang along.

I've never sung in the labyrinth before.
I was loud, bold, and perfectly in tune
with my mind's melody
that no one else could hear.

As I came, at last, back
to the entrance
my face was wet.

Dear World,
whatever I may have done
to deserve this moment
of peace, power, hope, and joy,
show me how to do more.

A sound not speech

On this steamy late August day,
I shouldn't pass up the chance to go to the river for a swim.
The water is low, the hour is late, and the air is hot and buggy.
But, the dogs are telling me we must go,
and I know that the days of visits to the swimming hole are numbered.
I grab my life vest, river shoes, walking stick and we're off.

Heavenly, that's how it is. The water is cool,
running low over the rocks and noisy.
I stand knee-deep at the edge of the drop-off of the swimming hole,
spread my arms and do one of those Trust Falls,
trusting the water to catch me.
Then we three dog-paddle together, swimming in community.
A few leaves are starting to fall in the water,
and the flow has slowed so it's easy to travel, no fighting the current.
Around and back, a rest on the log that juts
from the center of the swimming hole,
two more laps and we're done and homeward. I'm hungry.

Walking back toward the house,
something distracts the dogs in the woods, so
I am in the lead as we head out into the field.
So it is my footstep that startles them up out of the grass.

The pair of monarch butterflies rises right in front of me,
 twirling and flirting and touching and parting,
dancing together up to my nose and then
away, across the weeds and grass.
Their orange blazing against the green.

A sound comes out of me,
comes out of somewhere deeper than my throat.
 It is a sound not speech, more like song.
It is my heart leaping out of my mouth.

Rescue

I ask the world
to save me

I ask
the fields of beans
the trees and flowers
the bug that lands on my chest
and looks up at my face
with infinitely faceted eyes

I ask the river
each stone, each leaf
and the water singing
along its path

I ask the sun
the sky
to save me
once again

Save me
help me to swallow
or heave
this lump in my throat

this lump that won't
move
to become a sob
or a scream

*

sunlight dances
on the river
like fireworks
starlight

resting on a rock
amidst the gurgle
a heron feather

I tuck it in my hair
and breathe

what we are made of

skin and bones
fingernails, hair
protons and other invisibles
clusters of cells with a common purpose

the life force, whatever that is

hope and love
want, hunger, foolishness
leftovers and dog hair and dust
ideas, worries, regrets

water mostly

fear, surprise, sweat
shortcomings and moments of ecstasy
thirst, tears, shadows
promises, kept and broken

love, and again love

the beat that compels us to dance
and the pull that makes plants reach for the light
stardust and secrets
electricity, magic, music

connections

the found, the kept, the given away
waste and desire
laughter, whispers, shouts
blood and sap

stories

butter and pies and gravy
hushed lovemaking in a place called home

sweetness, salt
daughters and sons

sun

rain and dirt and wind
leaves, feathers, stones

Laurie Lambert was born and raised in West Springfield, Massachusetts, the middle child of three sisters. After studying chemistry at Williams College, she continued her education at the University of Wisconsin-Madison and received a PhD in medical microbiology and immunology. Laurie's career as a research scientist studying inflammation, arthritis and asthma resulted in the publication of a dozen papers in scholarly journals.

Laurie and her husband Chris Kelling brought triplets into the world in 1994. Not long after, Laurie cut back to part-time scientist. She eventually left her research career to become a full-time Mom to Claire, Hannah and Owen, and a substitute teacher in their school district.

As the triplets transitioned to college, Laurie began to pursue an interest in writing. She enrolled in core classes at Women Writing for (a) Change in Cincinnati and eventually attended their Conscious Feminine Leadership Academy. Currently, Laurie is a certified facilitator at WWf(a)C and leads weekly writing classes. She is also a member of the Greater Cincinnati Writer's League. Laurie has become an enthusiastic activist through the V-Day organization, whose aim is the prevention of violence toward women and girls. She organizes an annual V-Day event with WWf(a)C in support of this cause. Laurie and Chris, her husband of 30 years, have spent the majority of their married life at the family farm on Todd's Fork of the Little Miami River. In 2013, Laurie and her family built an eleven circuit Chartres Labyrinth in the barnyard.

Laurie's poems have been published in *Labyrinth Pathways, Annapurna, Clarify, Common Threads, The Sycamore,* and *For a Better World*. Finishing Line Press published her first chapbook, *What I Can Carry*, in 2016.

www.ingramcontent.com/pod-product-compliance
Lightning Source LLC
Chambersburg PA
CBHW070549090426
42735CB00013B/3125